D0529409

cartooning for kids!
MEAN 'N' MESSY
monsters

By Dave Garbot

This library edition published in 2015 by Walter Foster Jr.,
an imprint of Quarto Publishing Group USA Inc.
6 Orchard Road, Suite 100
Lake Forest, CA 92630

Distributed in the United States and Canada by
Lerner Publisher Services
241 First Avenue North
Minneapolis, MN 55401 U.S.A.
www.lernerbooks.com

First Library Edition

Library of Congress Cataloging-in-Publication Data

Garbot, Dave.
  Mean 'n' messy monsters / by Dave Garbot. -- First Library Edition.
      pages cm. -- (Cartooning for kids!)
  ISBN 978-1-939581-48-8
1. Monsters in art--Juvenile literature. 2. Drawing--Technique--Juvenile literature. I. Title. II. Title: Mean and messy monsters.
  NC825.M6G37 2015
  741.5'1--dc23

                                                    2014017647

9 8 7 6 5 4 3 2

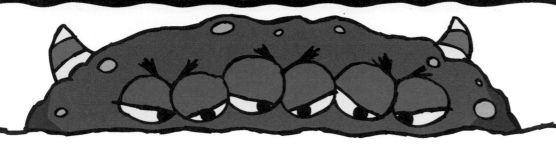

Table of Contents

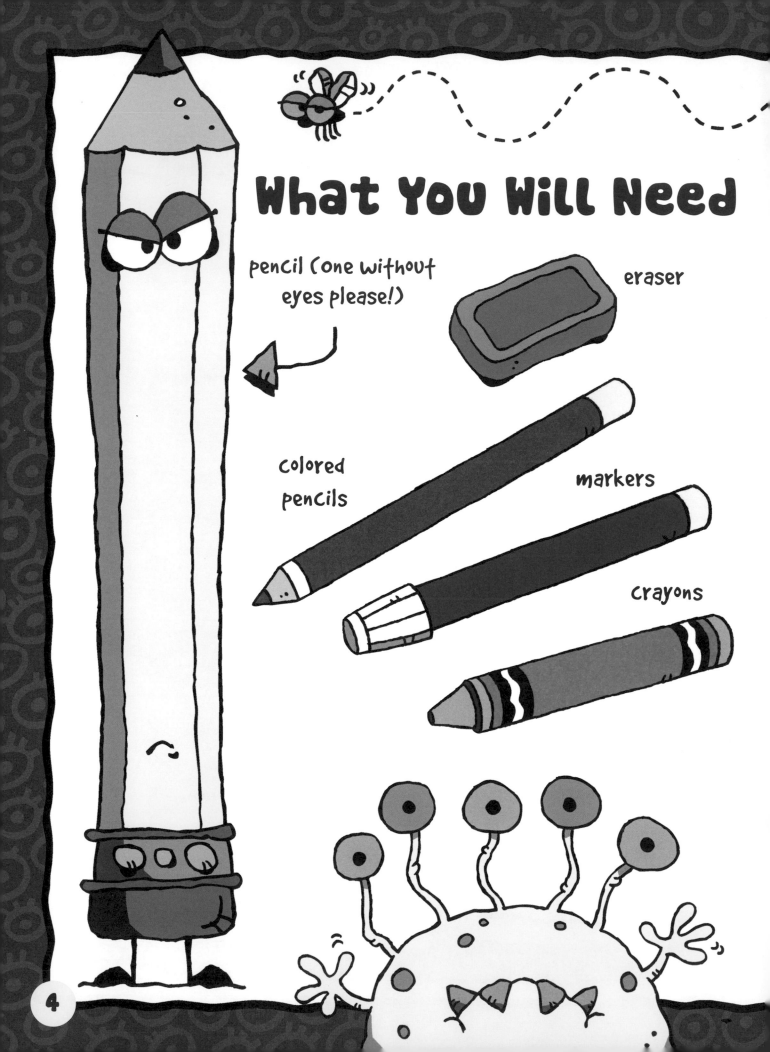

What You Will Need

pencil (one without eyes please!)

eraser

colored pencils

markers

crayons

Getting Started

Our first drawing lesson is about to begin, and that can be kind of scary if you're first starting out. Don't worry about how nice your drawing looks or whether your lines are perfectly straight. When drawing monsters, the messier and squigglier the better! Follow the steps and your monster will appear right before your very eyes (or eye)!

The Monster Shop

Hello. I'm Ignatius, but you can call me Iggy. I work here in The Monster Shop to keep the things you may need when drawing your "friends." Look around and use anything you like. If you don't like it you can always bring it back, or better yet, just erase it! Good luck!

Eyes

Noses

Ears

Mouths

Feet

 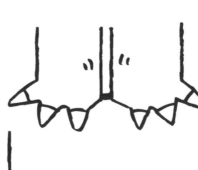 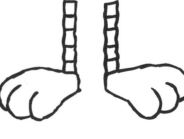

 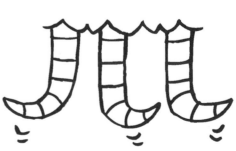

Unique Monsters

Monsters come in all shapes and sizes. They may hide under beds, in closets, or even under cereal bowls—they're crazy! You should know that mean 'n' messy ones have serious attitude problems too. They always seem to be grumpy, even though they look funny and make us laugh! As you draw your monsters, try to think like one. It will help your creatures take on personalities only you can give them, which will make them special! Grab your pencil and give us a growl (maybe just a small one), and let's have some fun!

Stinky Foot

Pee-yew! Start out with a simple rectangle-like shape, and then add details with each step!

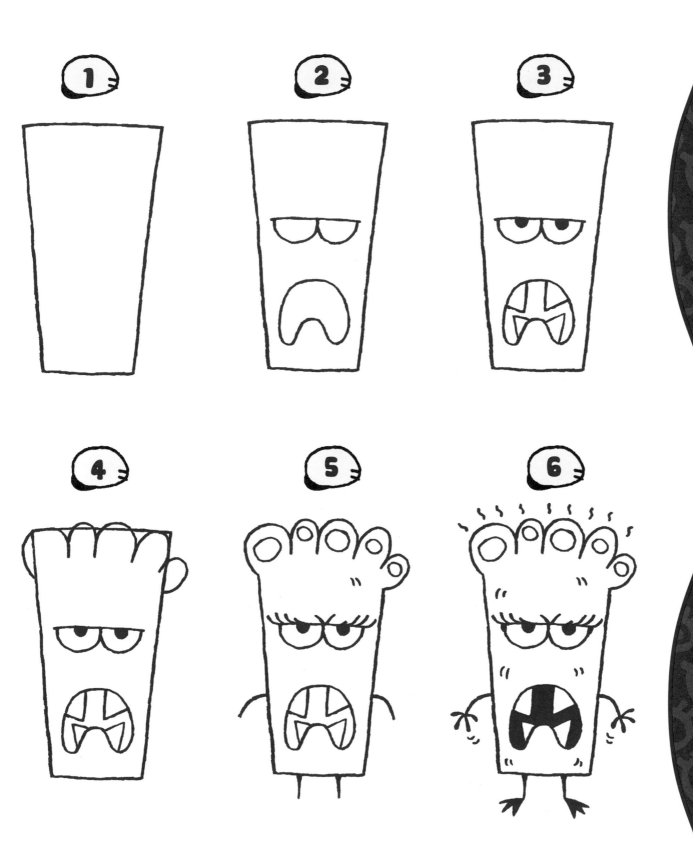

Sparky

Sparky is not your normal house pet.
How do you think he would look with one eye—or maybe three?!
If you need some ideas, go back to page 8 and visit Iggy.

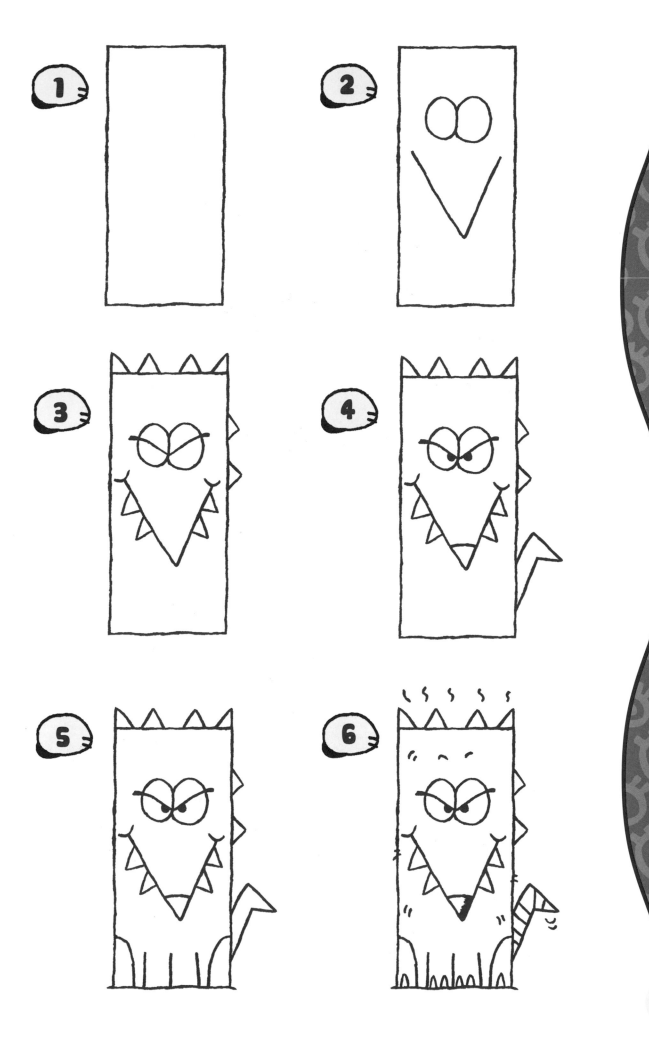

15

Sluggy

Slugs? Extremely disgusting, but with all those eyes...yikes!
How would he look with a nose?

Spidey

Spidey has decided to wear a hat, but you can take it off if you like or give him a different one. Do you have a favorite kind of hat that you would like him to wear?

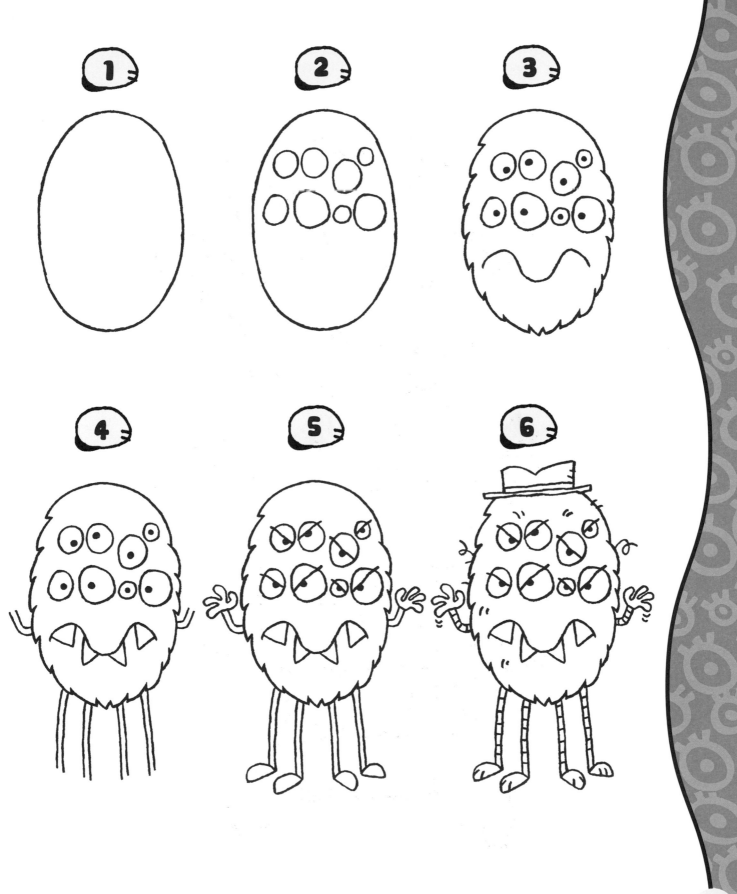

Fingers

This monster has five fingers, but maybe you would like him to have more—or less?

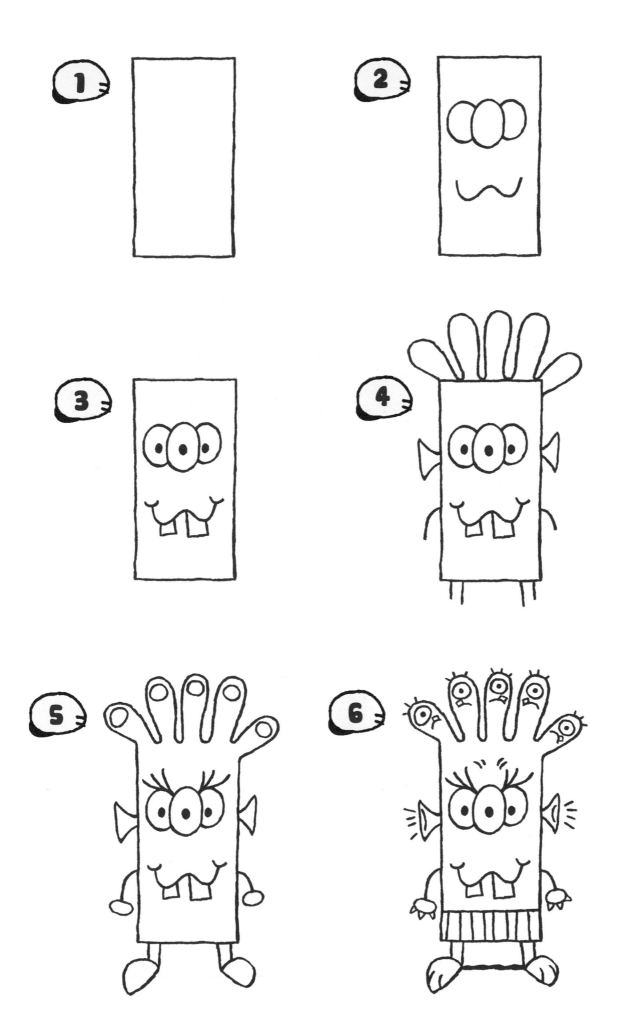

Lil' Devil

Lil' Devil looks like a handful! What if there were more than one of him?! Maybe you can give him a few "friends" on your page.

Harry

Harry does not look happy at all. Maybe he'd feel better with a different mouth—or maybe with a nose?

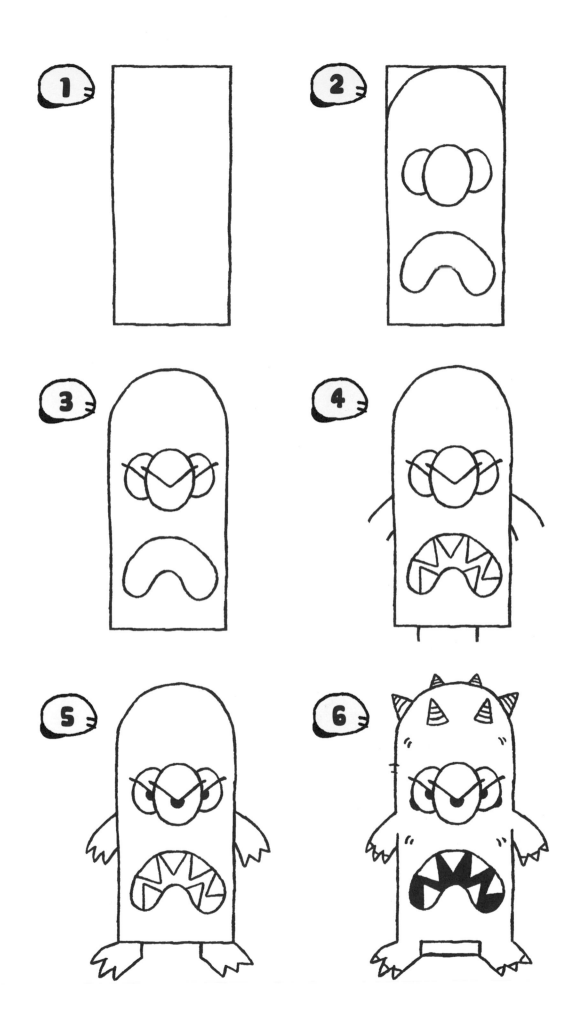

Birdo

Birdo looks pretty hip with his hat, but try drawing him without it. What do you think he looks like under his lid?

Marcia

How do you think Marcia would look with one eye or a different nose? Go back to Iggy if you need some ideas!

29

Obot

Obot is a wacky-looking robot as it is.
What if he had more arms or eyes? Yikes!

space Kitty

Ick! Space Kitty is making a mess inside the spaceship.
Can you draw Kitty without the drool and with a different mouth?

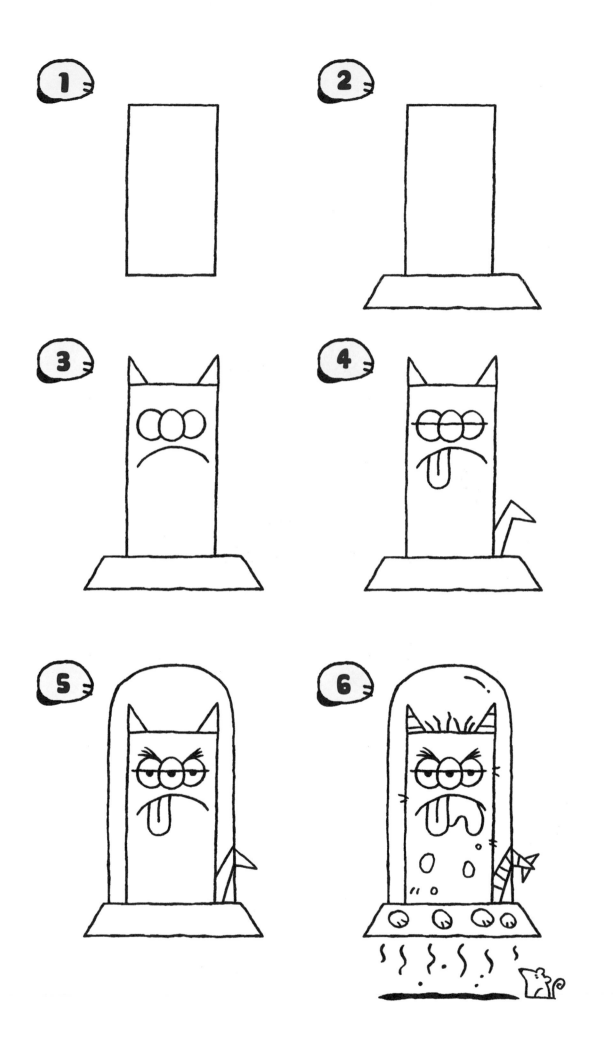

33

Mertle

Can you draw three more Mertles,
each one a little different from the others?

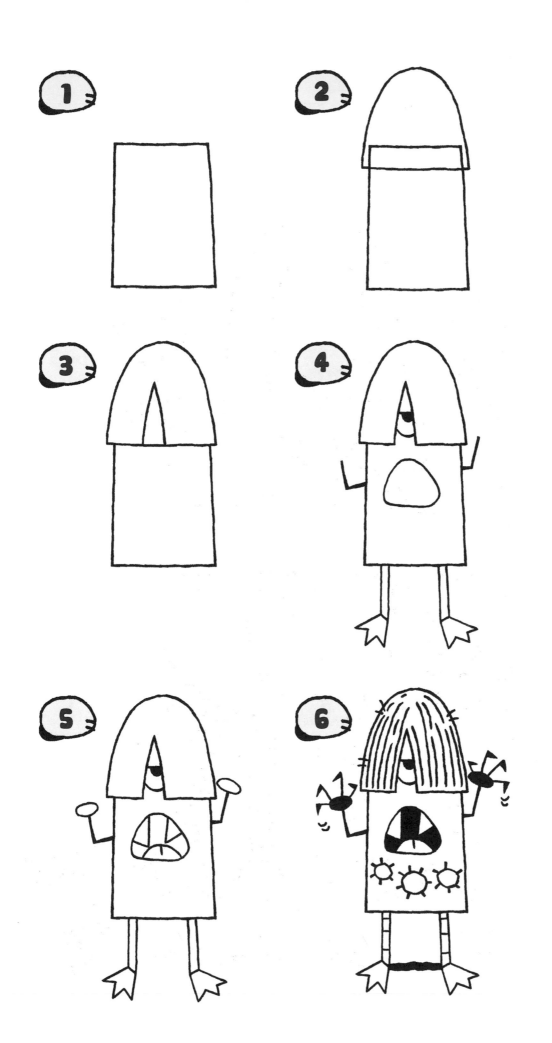

Chompers

Chompers is pretty creepy! Can you add more arms, eyes, and maybe even more teeth?

Honker

Honker has a crazy-looking nose, but maybe you can change that. Go back to Iggy and see what you can find...or make one up!

Fishy

Fishy likes to eat worms. Yuck! Can you
add a few coming out of his mouth to make him happy?

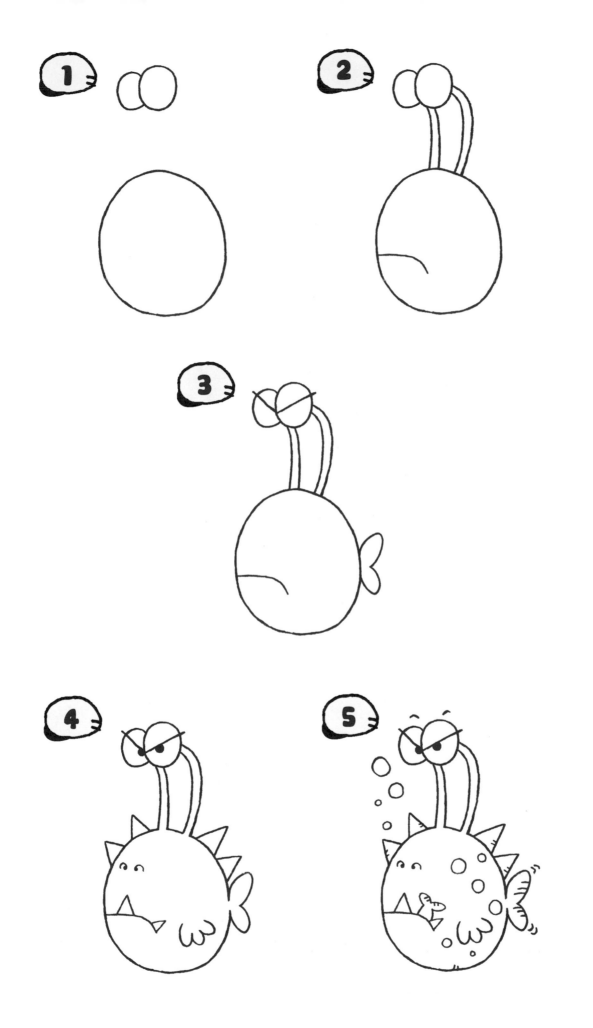

Hopper

This is one weird rabbit. How would he look with four ears?
What if he only had one eye...or maybe three?

Squiddy

Holy calamari! That's a funny-looking squid.
Let's change his mouth. Go ask Iggy if you need an idea.

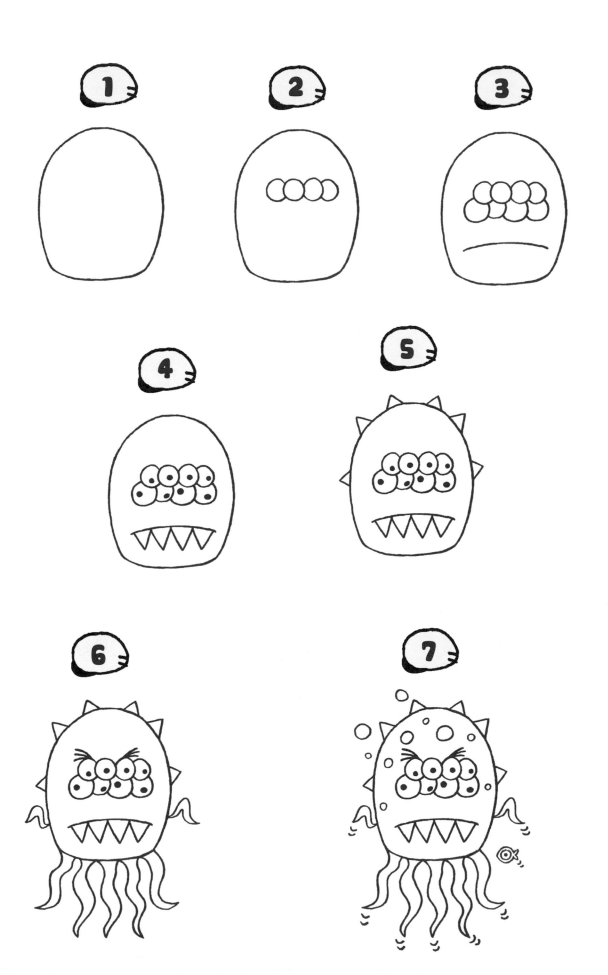

3-Eye

OOh! All those teeth are pretty scary. How different would 3-Eye look if you gave him a new mouth? Would he seem as mean?

46

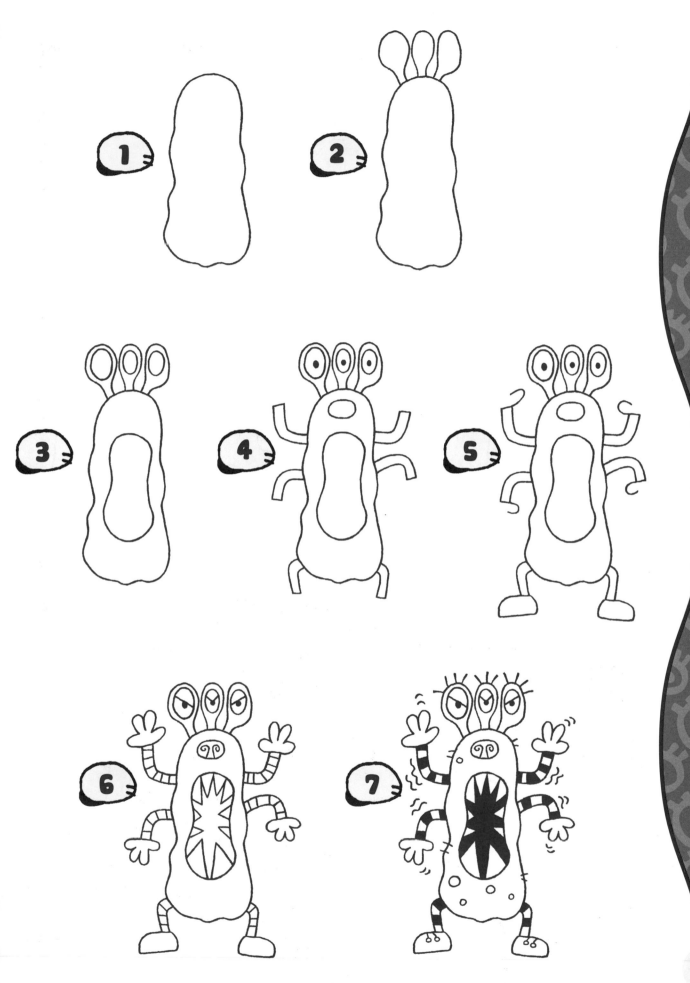

47

Famous Monsters

As mentioned before, monsters come in all different shapes and sizes. You never know what they're going to look like! But some monsters are really famous. In fact, some of these "celebrities" seem like they've been around forever—they've even been in movies and on TV! In this section, you'll learn to draw some of these famous monsters step by step. Maybe you can add a few extra touches to make them your own unique monster stars!

Monster X-ING

King Kong

Uh-oh...King Kong looks a little upset. Go back to page 8 and try a different mouth and ears on the King! That might calm him down.

Godzilla

When you're done, try coloring Godzilla a different color.
Maybe give him some spots too!

Wilma the Witch

Wilma has a pointy hat, but would she still look like a witch with a square one? Change up her wardrobe and experiment!

Frankie

Frankie is wearing his sneakers, but how would he look if you took his shoes off and added different feet? Go see Iggy if you need ideas!

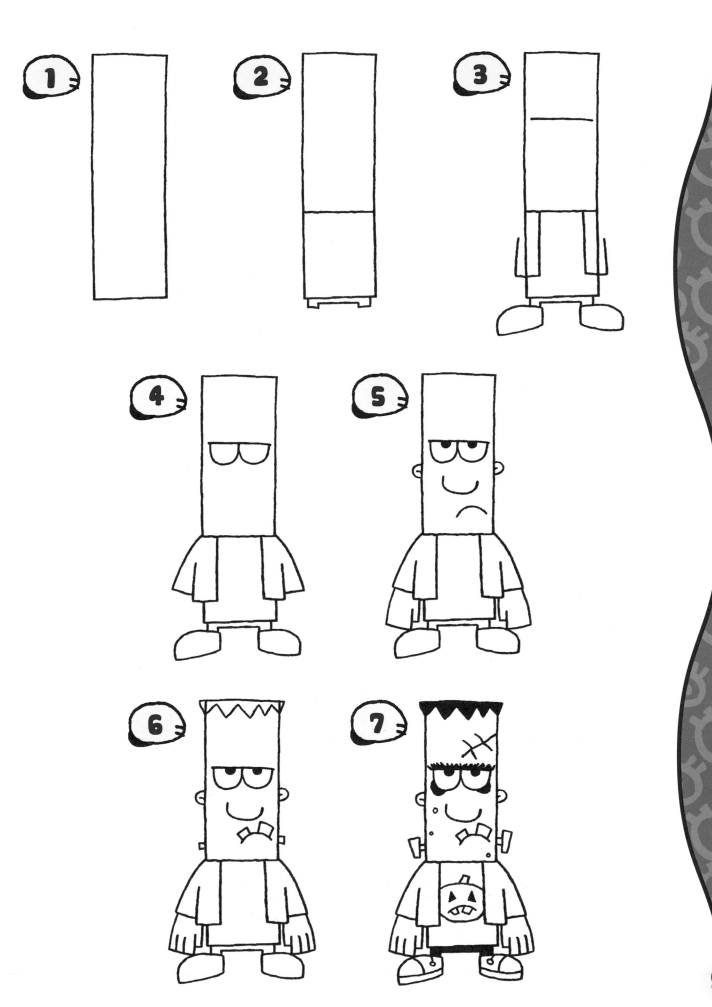

Draco

Draco looks pretty spiffy in this tuxedo. He must be going to a party! Add another character to your drawing so he won't have to go alone! How about a party hat too?

Oh, Mummy

Mummy looks unhappy. How would he look if you covered his mouth or changed his teeth? Would he still look mean?

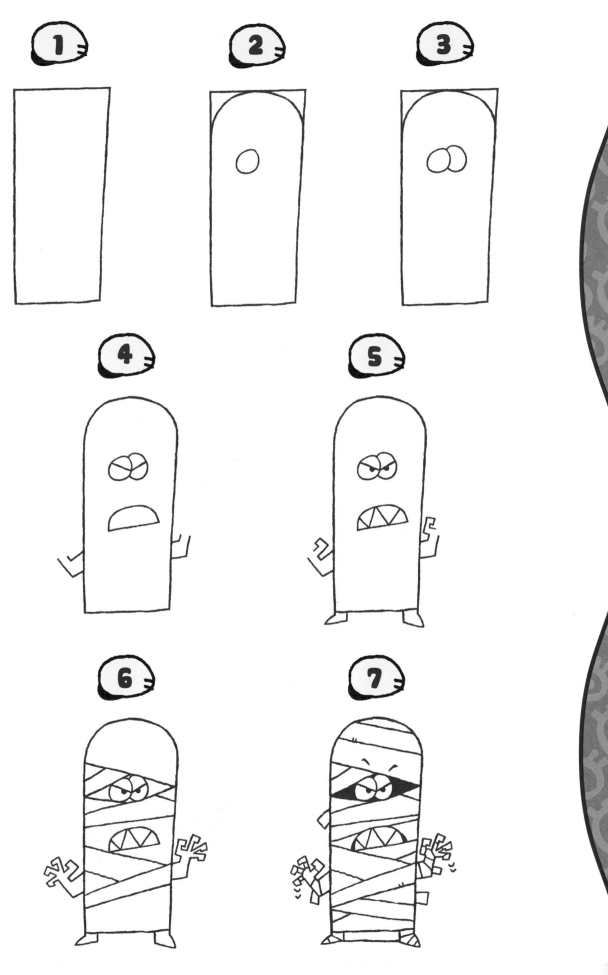

zombie Mike

Mike looks pretty dapper in his bow tie. Return to The Monster Shop on pages 8-9 and find him some crazy feet!

63

About the Author

Dave Garbot is a professional illustrator and has been drawing for as long as he can remember. He is frequently called on to create characters for children's books and other publications. He always has a sketchbook with him, and he gets many of his ideas from the things he observes every day, as well as from lots of colorful childhood memories. Although he admits that creating characters brings him personal enjoyment, making his audience smile, feel good, and maybe even giggle is what really makes his day.